MW00458858

UGLY DUCKLING PRESSE
LOST LITERATURE SERIES

Eleni Vakalo

BEFORE LYRICISM

This translation is based on the following editions:
Το δάσος (Καραβία, 1954), Τοιχογραφία (Οι φίλοι της λογοτεχνίας,
1956), Ημερολόγιο της ηλικίας (Δίφρος, 1958), Περιγραφή του
σώματος (Δίφρος, 1959), Η έννοια των τυφλών (1962), Ο τρόπος να
κινδυνεύουμε (1966)

Lost Literature Series #18

ISBN 978-1-937027-70-4
First Edition, First Printing, 2017

Ugly Duckling Presse
The Old American Can Factory
232 Third Street #E-303
Brooklyn, NY 11215
www.uglyducklingpresse.org

Distributed in the USA by SPD/Small Press Distribution
Distributed in Canada (via Coach House Books) by Raincoast Books
Distributed in the UK by Inpress Books

Cover art by Nina Papaconstantinou ("St. John, Apocalypse," 2004)
Design and typesetting by goodutopian and Don't Look Now!
The type is Adobe Garamond Pro and Univers 57

Offset printing and binding by McNaughton & Gunn
Covers printed offset at Prestige Printing
Cover paper donated by Materials for the Arts

This book was made possible in part by a grant from the National
Endowment for the Arts and by public funds from the New York
City Department of Cultural Affairs in partnership with the City
Council, as well as continued support from the New York State
Council on the Arts.

Eleni Vakalo

BEFORE LYRICISM

TRANSLATED FROM THE GREEK
BY KAREN EMMERICH

LOST LITERATURE SERIES #18
UGLY DUCKLING PRESSE
BROOKLYN, NY

Contents

THE FOREST

Poetic Fiction

(in the style of an expressive ballet)

1954

The shape of the forest has
The shape of a jellyfish
That you catch in your hands and it slips through
As a wave
Pushes it out
Perhaps this happens
Because
It moves
Without
Opening seashores
That are white
And
The fresh ones glisten
While the others
Are white all through
You'll find too the bones of the drowned

Now I'll push out my heart
But no
Since jellyfish
Have no blood

If I pretended for so long to be writing poems, it was only so I
could speak of the forest.

At night people betray one another
And when the forest
Begins
To smother you
You cry out
As if
You were not in
The forest

The forest is like my nights
Which as dawn comes
Are not at all
The same
The forgotten dead
Whom alone we set aside
Near-dead advance
With startling movements
Or
—We'd like to imagine—
A single
Detail
In daylight it's green
So the forest
Is a forest
With trees.

EPISODE ONE

MY FATHER'S EYE

My father had a glass eye.

On Sundays when he stayed home he would take other eyes from his pocket, shine them with the cuff of his sleeve and call my mother over to choose. My mother would laugh.

In the mornings my father was pleased. He would roll the eye around in his palm before putting it in and call it a good eye. But I didn't want to believe him.

I would wrap myself in a dark shawl as if I were cold but really I was keeping watch. Finally one day I saw him cry. It was no different from a real eye.

This poem
Is not for those to read
Who don't love me
Or even
Those
Who won't know me
If they don't believe I existed
As
They did

After the story with my father I was suspicious
even of those whose eyes were real.

They found the bird killed
In the forest
So small
If you compare it
To the space all around
Where the cries of the frightened
Couldn't penetrate

> *Short dialogue*
> *That arrives, closely following the circle*
>
> *—Did you love her?*
> *—Oh, no*
>   *Back then*
>   *Hats with big feathers*
>   *Were all the rage*
> *—Swallows?*
> *—Lord, no*
>   *Salamanders*

Do you really know whether you're inside or out
Of the closed spaces that always exist?
It depends entirely
On the slant of the sun
Even at the seaside
On Sunday excursions
In rowboats
While around them
Huge ships steam off
A whole fleet
With us in their wake

Like children's prams being taken
From the park
At dusk
Leaving our hands
This feeling of our hands grasping
As they rest on benches
The dew painted
Not only
In the forest

EPISODE TWO

THE SWINEHERD
OR, THE BEGGARS' SONG

When Odysseus on landing moved toward the forest from the shore, he found his comrades seated in a line each with open eyes watching him and singing with a hand outstretched along the seaside road.

The mice drowned in spring
Dragging by the tail
The old and the young
The blind who didn't understand
And all those who sat on the church steps
And begged
Good sir a little help please

Here where you pass passed they
Who will drown

And they began their chorus again:

When after the encounter Odysseus returned he joined them as the last in line, since he had no more need to be clever, thus moving nearer to the forest than the shore.

The swineherd had sold his pigs
Made a bed from their hides
And slept
Good sir
A little help
Please

Clipping from Kathimerini

In Norway a mass suicide of rodents was observed; during a
certain season they cast themselves in herds into the sea.

Leaving behind the dense forests of Scandinavia

    But Greece is what I knew
    And its landscape
    At the moment I committed suicide
    Was dawning
    As if I were emerging free
    From the waters
    And the forests shone
    Dewdrops falling
    As a warm breeze rustled the leaves
    Forests full of light
    Bodiless
    Of lean pines
    Blazing
    With glints
    Of sun on the rocks
    That tumble to the shore

Time passes
And the shade in the clearing multiplies
(There are other forests of firs
And chestnuts
On the banks of the Peneus)
Slanted at first
It divides
The trunks on the right side of the circle
If it were two woodcutters sawing
The trees would fall booming
To the earth
Later turning from trunk to trunk
It fleetingly touches the trees on the other side
Before they are all sunk in darkness
Together
During that brief spell is when you hear the birds chirp

So what they say
That in the forests the birds sing all day
Is a lie
The forests are ruled by fear
And the beasts
And birds
Know how to fear
Before they are born

(Excerpt from another poem)

… As for instance that beast
Torn by the teeth of the trap's jaws
Struggling to get free
Ignores the blood
And fears other traps as it hides in the shadows
Before it escapes …

This poem never took a finished form
But I put it here
In a likeness of forest
It too a likeness—the best I can give—of inscriptions
"In memoriam"
They erect in the forests
When shade cooled the statues
And those walking on the riverbanks
And the seaside places
Perhaps because we find the inscriptions shattered

EPISODE THREE

THE EAVESDROPPER

When people similarly engaged thronged together
Forgetful of the forests
The eavesdropper would try to guess
How each spent his nights

He was a person who liked history. He even liked to wander at
night through parks
                        Full of whisperings
because he suspected that love wasn't just what he had known
it to be.

The occasions for this man were never enough

I saw him reeling with exhaustion face buried in his hands
because he never gathered from the debris all he had imagined.

And that noise you hear in the forest
Concentrating hard
When no one else can guess
Of those coming for the first time
And the blood symmetrically starts to rise
An echo of things to come
Like a bow whose string
Is stretched taut
The arrow back toward the warrior's chest
Before the conflict
With small steps I pull back
Recognizing the harmony in the fear of this moment

Comment A

In that case we must describe how everyone was afraid. For a woman it is natural to experience also a pleasure in fear.

Comment B

Sometimes a realized pleasure defines existence to a point past what consciousness can grasp.

Comment C

If our age were not ruled by fear—a feminine feeling—the poetess might have relied more heavily on the lyric element, more in keeping with her position, as one for whom composition does not come naturally. (I would like to rest.) Whereas here she feels she is not the only one who fears.

He called to me with a beast's voice in the night
He called for me
Oh come, come

.

Continuation of the eavesdropper

As he passed us, he heard me speaking to him of the child and
of everything else that had happened that day.
I don't know whether he also heard the sobs.

The forest
Always took
The shape
Of the shadow he cast
As he passed
Between
The trees
Of the forest
And the color changes
Of their shadows
On the roots below

But surely I wasn't to blame
Because now
When I think of the time
When I ran
The next day
To hide
It was strange
How the sea
Touches
The forest's edge

EPISODE FOUR

I weep over the body
of a sleeping child for
I feel I will betray him
before a new day dawns.

Let my confession
Be written for the first time
With its true name
Confession
And not an attempt at poetry
Since that's how it must be
I must hurt even more

Once I could protect myself
Now I call it solitude

Related to this, I'll add to my memories that I once had a dog.
I thought there could be nothing better than to be a dog. The
way you hit them and they submit.

It's been a long time since then.

As for what I've left
Today
For you to understand
It wasn't from love
It was because
One can drown in the forest
And I only wanted
To find a way out

(Pause for deep breath)

This poem
Is my last revolutionary act
Before I obey
The advice of foreigners.

January – February 1952

PLANT UPBRINGING

1956

Plants have a different upbringing from people
Not moving isn't unique to them
Nor is not committing suicide
Plants are perpetual revolutionaries
Just think how they grow during the hour of the moon

The hour of the moon
The expanse
Of desert
Where grasses
Cropped at the edges
Seem to recede
Resembling boats
At the coast
The boats further down
Yet the shore appears
As if it
Not they
Were difficult to reach

Another hour of the moon
When the women grow numerous
Seated together
On peaks
There
Where the downward slope begins
Of the hills—not high
Their bodies
Seem tangled in the moonlight
Just as smooth

because often plants
chiefly in humid places of constant growth
clambering one on the next
support the ascent of branches that soar up high
and then younger ones bend back down
with shoots green to the root
and tender
first with fuzz
then full of sap
those are more difficult to break
or you'll hear a crack
though you thought it would take time to conquer this plant
it produces a pleasure
unquestionably plants support one another

The pleasure of breaking plants
Most likely it's the influence of the accumulate moon
At that time of month when it reflects
In a shape smaller but precise
A circle of shore the sea at first conceals
Then as it recedes in the evening
The sand shows us at its edge
The shape of the day to come

(I'm talking about the thing that stirs inside movements)
the way
the leaves of a plant are always more transparent at their edge
and its body slowly slowly from the center spreads
in some it proceeds by being torn
otherwise it might not reach

those are the largest
called philodendrons
leaftrees
when their time comes to dry they begin again from the tips
Plants are monsters
with monstrous legs
Only their movement is stationary

Ficus gravidumbra
This one gives mostly a sense of fear
Perhaps you've noticed how its leaves
Are able to absorb the breeze
And don't move at all when during siesta
It blows cool
That's why they say its shade is heavy
The fig tree always reminds us of hanged men
Not because of Judas
Likely they only imagined Judas hung himself
From this tree
So as to have a believable hanged man
But mostly because of its color
As if—pulling at its scars—they've turned
Its skin inside out
Where there are knots this feeling is stronger
Because it appears from inside
As if the skin is right where it splits
And you notice even more
How pulling it out
It dries at once in the air

Not all plants are like this
Now let's turn to the plants in the garden

The plants in the garden
Give a first impression
Of peace
Even more so than pets
But that impression changes
As evening falls
And the garden seems to have multiplied
In the movement
Of proportions of shapes
You understand
At such times I try not to look
In case someone is hiding there
As it often seems
Though in morning the garden
Will be once more
Like the slanting line on the cheeks
Of very young girls
When the light strikes them from the side

We have gardenias in our garden
At first they have to grow
Covered with a drinking glass
I've never tried letting them be
I'm always afraid
They might not take

I speak on this subject because I want to be
Against:
> Humor
> Grace
> Personal consistency
> The spirit
> As understood by European civilization
This is our chief difference from plants

The bushy plants we have by our beaches
Are perhaps the only ones that resemble us
Tender weeds sprout among them
Descending the hills to the sea
Peacefully neighboring a cluster of bushes
Our plants that open with a growth the climate makes mild
Like nests
They hide their shade at their deepest point
And turn a color darker than other plants
On their branches a gorgeous red
Only when they are shoots
Do they sway in the breeze
Like tassels
Or remind me of a smile
When they've grown sturdier
Their bark smells if you scratch it
But not their leaves
Though if you crush them they do

At night the breath of plants
Freezes around the moon

Which habits of plants frighten me
When shoots burst from dry branches
folded inside are tiny green leaves
—Perhaps that's why you can't ever be sure a plant
is really dead—
because a new stalk
strong
and blooming
sprouts from the very root
replacing the withered trunk
other plants drop seed before they die
in the proper season you'll see them sprout
or the root remains
and the next year will give us more and fuller

The endurance of plants astonishes me
Some slip their roots beneath the foundations
Advancing beside the garden
A poplar sprouted that way by the house and grew big
You can't hem plants in
You just prune them when necessary
Those plants we all think so simple

The seasons when habits change
Affect the skin
And when you close your eyes you feel more deeply
How you will change landscapes
Once the invisible internal movements in the bark begin
As when you're close to the sea
But the curve in the road still hides it

Descending
The breeze first brings you the sea's salty tang
The breeze that comes
To our touch has first touched
The things and shapes of the sea
Yet descending to the beach
They appear to you suddenly
That's how I feel when I see
Plants open abruptly one day to the next

Most likely the sensation
In uncovered seasons
Includes also the shapes
Of our dead bodies

I move on through the landscape of cacti
It rots in that place
Denied entry
And the drive to infiltrate upward
So as simply to demand
Breathing room as it grows
In a crowd of others
At a body's height
Which juiceless remains slight
The cactus
Has gone softer and easier to approach

They resemble reptiles more

DIARY OF AGE

1958

STILLNESS

Is the safeguarding by silence
Of a low land
Its age still insatiable
Lying deeply in wait
—Against the attraction of another planet—
There where the older works
Sank into its body

The works are

Stranded dangers from various eras
The column drums—vertebrae—resemble
White plumeless birdheads
Like broken halves of other animals' skulls
Which if you find them remind you
Of shards of old limestone carvings
Though you won't find birdbones on these rocky shores
They must crumble quickly
Since eating them when they're small
They even melt in your mouth.

The flavors are strange and persist
Igniting the signs in the sun.

MYTHOLOGY OF TASTES

—Mostly they aren't from birds—

The fish's diaphanous embryo
Passes milky and unchanged into the light
Too small to have shape
And it doesn't cause fear
If swimming you see down below the dark
Shape of the fish
It doesn't matter that it slips from your touch
Slightly denser than the taste of the sea
Amassing the sea
It struggles to expel
As it slowly takes shape
Later it plays
In moments of stillness it leaps from the water
Shimmering
As if the sea were tasting the sun again.

BY NATURE THE ORGANISM RETURNS

In the low land we spoke of
The marshland of Delos
—The sea still hangs from the disk of a dead planet—
The mud is slow
And forms an ashen crust when it dries
The water remains within
And the wind
Whatever wind was shut in as it passed
Through the old roads carrying scents
From the whole sea
The oaks on the opposite shore
And the ruins
Of the footsteps
That once sounded
From the terraces where people strolled
It took their gentle voices

Foundered by decay.

Some are not wholly able
Like shadowy membranes
Like jellyfish halfway down in the water
They change
Interrupting their sinking to return
It is fearful to admit.

Thus in this muddy land
With rocks and unkempt weeds in the riverbed
With another stride, in another time, entwine
The limbs of those who remained
Whatever limbs remained of those people
Frogs and snakes
Severed worms that sprout another body
Slowly slowly
The skulls and shin bones
Blackened where the dog once bit them.

DIGRESSION ABOUT THE DOG

The observation in very slow time
As in poems slowly slowly the words entwine
Of the variants
That static in the end remain
As the odor remains on corpses
When quickly they turn again
And the roots in the soil make more acrid
Its own particular odor
Ambling at a distance from the unknown hunter
Showing now and then through the trees
The dog runs deeper
Then returns
A dog with straight lids
Is the one that guides the gun.

SOMETIMES the poet cannot abstract shapes
From the crowd
—Beggars and merchants moving early in the morning
On a festival day
Shoving and cursing to get
The best spots
On the shores of Delos
And the ship's prow gleamed gold from afar
From that far the Romans would be glad
To see it like a bowl whose water has run dry
And octopi and fish and other sea creatures
Hit the bottom and turn all together—
Whatever survives there
                Which afterward the poems
                        Constantly approaching
Like shades
Like thickenings of wind
Like rags of shades they pine
Lamenting on the ground round a pit
They leave
Then come again
Digging with their nails
For whatever might offer
A sign of help from the crowd.

There is a tragedian amid the silence.

SLIPPING the silence
In the shape of an eel or the long new spine of a fish
As it neatly slides past its flanks
Toward the back and closes again at the end
The sea undisturbed by the foreign motion
Of the fish that swim in the sea
When a man about to swim
Stands naked before it
In the light
The light flows
Into the motion happening within him
It travels from the sun
To new suns on each shore
Beautiful summer
The hottest and longest of all seasons.

The most lovely body taking shape in silence
I remember its limbs following one on the next
As if some new manner had caused it
To be born again.

FROM THE SEA the sea turtle
Climbing with ease
Is buoyed by the waters
A swarm of fish small and gold
Darting quickly fan out
Around the hook like a star
There are so many
Like splinters of life
Extending a part of their flesh
There are others
With no mouths or eyes
That simply cover the food they need

I CONSIDER how fitting to our works today
Is the genre of the polyp
                              Since
In such a way will events unfold
Leaving foreign layers
Calcic shells
Dried bits of sponge
Or branches dropped from above
By weary passing birds
Dead organisms in the sea
Enter the union of sinews
And join together
Forming vertebrae from empty broken shells
That pass into other branches
The salt accumulates
Seaweed ossifies then shatters as its whirls
The print remains
In whiter striations these petrifications permeate
Bulges, leaving empty spaces
Where marine reptiles nest
And barnacles
And the last pieces to stick
Still sway at the edges, back and forth in the water.

The conquest of the space in the joints
Always sounds silent in poems, like a crack.

DIGRESSION ABOUT THE SPIDER

Striking the spider
The spasm as it falls
And its legs contract and tangle
In three closed corners
The whole spider shrinking
Death when it suddenly comes
With a swift pain from the strike
And that power you have in your hands
The image of these moments gathers
As passing you saw it on the wall
Creeping with its eight legs
In an odd rhythmic arrangement
The rapid change
In the scene, starting with the strike,
Transforms the innocent into intent.

THE SCARCENESS OF WATER

Thirst begins as pleasure
And the lips swell
In a texture that once lushly had
Other curves
And a different way of asking
The body's sufficiency exhausting
The smallest reserves of cool moments
In waterless lands
With quick feet creatures like gray fish
Parched of color
Dried and drained of blood
With quick eyes scurry
Fleeing into holes in the sand
Left in the seafloor's skin
With pores mostly open
You can't know what threat might arise
For those others
Where they survive
From creatures that hide
Waiting
Pincers or stingers ready
The blind gesture is astonishingly precise
Some are sucked

How suddenly they disappear
Bodies snapped
The sound dry, ghastly,
The food dry too
There is a way with a drop of water
Dissolving the body
To find
A laborious yield hidden from a merciless sun
—They cling thick on the lips
So sweet
These hard-won moments—
Offering sometimes their own lives
Tricking their blood, their saliva,
They make it food.

THE WATER

At the water's edge
The fish stirs
Old fearsome images sunk
In seaweed
In muddy sand
In cracks in the slimy rocks.

The fish: reptile
The fish: tongue of a hanged beast
Slaughtered, still holding that membrane
White cloudy fish washed up in the shallows.

DESCRIPTION OF THE BODY

1959

The body you see with simple limbs some knowing
what to call each separately, and together how they
pass in bands you hadn't noticed in motion, and other
points all over the body to which you've never given a
thought

Begetting an emotion
You no longer know it
As simply you knew it before

It is touch.
Watching, huge blind eyes graze the body, each naked
of its lid, whole, embeds in the body, watching after-
ward from there. Tranquil, soaked in itself, it doesn't
fight the body, but distracts
                              Taste from the mouth peels
                              The print off the palm
                              Draining sight from the gaze
             It is bad, doesn't feel
             our pain

First dance move

The body writhes
It doesn't suffer
It is the only thing
That in hurting
Feels pleasure

The body doesn't feel
Our pain
Bound
Ready and willing
It listens first
Wants to listen
Hollowing in its body
Constantly new
Chambers of hearing

Then it waits
More willing from fear
It multiplies it hides
In the depths of each chamber
More ready from fear
Willing
It anticipates the desire
That commands and
Brings that command
To motion

Dark dull hide of the prey still unconquered within us.

The body you see with simple limbs, some again at
rest, with slight constant tremors, the dull light bodies
collect and the other from the sun they hide, on days
that suddenly turn dark, conceives
    The great silent proliferations, in our sleep, of the
lives of leaves
    And those footprints that vanish as emerging from
the sea at noon you walk on the clean shore
                    At all hours our bodies
                    Sketch around us
                    Immense
                    Immense overlapping circles
                    Of the footprints of beasts

The body is calm, watching it seems fainted or asleep,
with eyelids gone white at the edges from the thick-
ening of light, sheltered, innocent, the body guards its
innocence always like a white wing

that comes to stroke
our hands over the blood when the cock writhes, that
little white bird

Second dance move

The trials take place in daylight
Beheadings always at night
Though at night
They cannot conceive
The eclipsing
Of blood by the white birds
Bodies are trees
Whole dark masses of light
Which when a breath
Of wind
Rushes through them
Storm trembling with it
As if it too
That breath of wind
Were closed
Within the body's
Shifting borders

"Prologue on the centaur pediment"
Would perhaps be a more suitable title for this poem

The great hymn that begins by naming things simply

How long can bodies not feel shame

How we exist is governed by how we take pleasure

First day of day
Of night
Of blood the distance suddenly sufficient
In the middle from the sun that empties
Opening a barbaric country
Slicing our country
As only a black sun can
And the day empties
Around the bodies no glow
From outside comes
But is left
            Awful—
Casting a barren splendor into the deep
Which has no surface
Nor like birds do they pass overhead
It now has bloomed green grass the green
Green shadow of thighs

Our hearts' surrender to tenderness brings a fear just as
sweet as muscles clenching before a threat

The bird
And the captive
Though more so the bird
Cupped in your hands
Both struggle at first
But in vain
To escape

Grasping the cock that little bird how the feel of it
changes, stroking the wing at its base up toward the belly

In vain
Dragging the wing far
To one side
The body crumples
Hits the earth
The startled captive bird
Has a heart frightened thus warm

See how the body, so gentle and vulnerable, now feels the sense of space within the shell of its own sky.

It is a monument, the body that swelled
In its nests
It brought landscapes and ruined mountains
It listened
Didn't listen to its voice
Didn't know if the voice was its own
Small black soil where it sat
On wounds you thought closed
Soon overtaken
By fragile white roots
Invisible white lives that crawled
Spread and crawled toward us
The movement was hushed
The body seemed still
Keeping watch
Though it tossed up birds
In the air above us we heard them leaving

There were other movements that didn't fool us
Slight propulsions of life
From its branches to the body's shadow
It turned
It was monstrously large
It had gods, hunters, and reptile eggs
Strangled prey they caught
And the others that fled into the forests
For them to come and catch
The body had multiplied and it wasn't good

The shadow we cast of its crying
Like a child's corpse or a newborn
Rested
On the slight shade of our shapes
     Which the heavenly phenomena define, these
days, always in corresponding succession.

Days the heavenly phenomena define in corresponding succession

Dedication to this place where the grass was left a bit brown

It passed running beside us, on a certain mission,
and turning slightly whispered
"We mustn't raise their suspicions.
We mustn't…"

                                        Without a sound
the wind in the space between the body and us

Description of the body

The body you see with simple limbs, some once more
at rest .   .   .
.   .   .   .   .

THE MEANING OF THE BLIND

1962

This wasn't the bird that would come
black and say "That is sun"
Its wings made no shadow
As I recalled
Only I knew it warm
Or cold embalmed

THE FIRST HOURS WHEN THE BLIND ENTER THE POEM

—From the diary of the poem—

They place me in a room

I can hear from the mass of silence that the endless night has
    not yet come
When I will walk through the door of the house before any-
    one can overtake me

One day I will find that door wide open, I will find out where
    it is,
as hugging the wall touching the objects one by one adjusting
    their positions I come to know them

Mostly I suspect before the bird comes like a clock to strike
    their names complete
—the bird a mere shape inscribed in their iron or wood—
I suspect that this time the way out must be somewhere close
    at hand

Does fear or what I'd learned to call pride forlornly call the
    empty bird, which comes only once I'm calm?

It will leave first
and when it spreads in the night its wings grow flesh where
    feathers will root, and in its chest the warmest weight,
and its outstretched neck will shape two true taut skins
as it travels again with the cry of other birds, of quick blood
it will wax in the tide of night

For before this our final endless night sank
The hilt
Of great comparisons
When above me beautiful birds cried
Covering the ruins
Carrying off dead fish
With their body the birds
Like a single driven shape
Drove
Rodents and fish
Still colored on their sloping sides
Only later did I realize they were frightful birds
Starting to peck at my eyes
Those who remember the cawing of birds
Will know what the birds meant

And parting around the children's knees like stones in a river
　　the water flowed
What place does hatred hold in my heart?

.

THEIR LEGEND

Panoplies will come from the new wind, banners from the old,
    seeds of necrophilous plants
                      From the river, from the sea
The fisherman with Assyria's stony death older in years than
    his civilization, outside of it, in the sand
And when his fish struggle to return, they cease

There is always a difference between a coolness one lives in
and that of the grave
Old and young sleepwalkers escape
Prophesying poems, without the tree's footstep they dream of
their branches
in their branches
During the month when birds pass they seek the bird of poetry
With each branch they are cooled with each bird they thirst
And in their voice a land will stand trembling from the colors
all over

He who measures in the alphabet of the floating cry the
people's passage into the desert

Like an upright staff before I slip danger sinks my voice,
    which is heard, will be heard each night through the
    openings of wind
and not even the cypress is wrapped so tightly in its body
    of shade
        it lives in that plain across the way
whose alluvial silts after the great green growth quietly up-
    turn the other face of the earth

Breasts heaped over time
And the white shields of the moons
Lie
Where hungry infants and dead lovers
On this edge of the abyss
With strange heads
Resurface

Exhausting in their tongue
The phrase that writhed
There they are again
When whisper and slight breeze
Nudged them to leave
Snakes scowling as they crawl
They return

With the snakes' golden eyes my eyes
Define a circle
As they waited for it to appear
The large bird
Floating
Perfectly balanced
In the air

RECOGNITION FROM THE SHADOWS

—or, in the large courtyard—

Around me as I sat in the yard and strange specks flew one
    by one from the shadows you couldn't say what or from
    where
a sudden commotion as if they all had risen at once, from
    my arms, my shoulders, leaving
and pairs of other birds in the crowd touched them with
    their beating wings

It was always evening and they were always restless before
    the light fell

Then for an instant they would appear like a sunlit field
where the flying pairs passed, specks of shadow knowing this
    way to move
                —those that had
left in the night and those I hid in thousands of cool nests—
the young and in love resting their shadows on their shadows
    as a slight shudder swept them off
toward the red hills that somewhere enclose the earth

THE BLIND MUST OFTEN TELL CHILDREN FAIRYTALES

In basement tunnels between the foundations of older
    houses is a building
Wounded and curled into the darkest corner dripping blood
    from its legs
Trembling from the pain in its flesh as its hard scales part
Hurting it more and more

Whiskers have sprouted on its face since the time
When a crowd brandishing sacrifices and banners flooded the
    space wildly with waves of music
Left its head on the altar
And in its place, on those butchered shoulders, put the head
    of a man

Now real tears wet its long beard
It hears the wind over the earth and far from the city's harbor
    the wave
It is the root of the great fire it feared, fingers scorched
And only as its wings filled and scattered did it hear them
    burning

It is a tattered bird, eaten by grief, old so old my likeness

If this poem filled with the beating of wings
It's because you hear birds
                    You don't just see them

I'll start now to send
Each night
                birds

It was the darkness and the great silent clot of wind that
    when it stands waiting is a dense king

And I had to visit the embassy of the unbridled where you
    sense but don't feel until the time comes

The wild bird drops onto the knees of the seated, the outside of
    lightning and above the rains, takes refuge with the one
    who knows white and black

I took refuge in the inaccessible as *a people in persecution*

But there was
        a time
                when the bones, great skeletons
of beasts and of birds, spread shining to the very tips
    of their wings
                steady and hovering
like wide chariots rising above the invading battle

The century struggled
A whirlwind of ash and dust
And dry salt
Articulated heaps sank their seated weight
Slowly into the clay

I remember it,
              great hovering birds
traversed their bodies
An exodus of fleeing deer swiftly passed
The burials
          —so many—
                    trees and dark animals
and during the chase newborns were left on their roots

The whole wind shook
Time trembling like foliage
Smelling like foliage
And trapped with it under the earth
Were many nests and souls of small animals

MY DOVE

Its feathers engulfed by hot blood
Sometimes cracking the window
                              Gently
The departing breeze takes one
Lays it on the grass with the dew
                    And sends it away
Death quivering with that heat
And it's barely dawn.

THE MEANING OF THE BLIND

—From the diary of the blind—

It spread like a shadow of threat and great calm, when you
    are inside it and there's no need to say
"when will it come"
a new adolescence whose grass, now I could look the sun full
    in the eye, sprouts black at its edges

As when awaiting love I feared for my heart
Many things vague around me and hearings more beautiful
As always when approaching silence the whispers and ges-
   tures you discern

All seemed to be vanishing then brightening again
Nostalgia for a slow metamorphosis accompanies the poem
For how did desire enter the poem and those things that
   ready death?

A deep contemplation puts them to rest

Deserted bands that glint, which unhindered winds sweep
   over the earth

With its naked head and quick small high cries
Of the throat
Crossing—so quickly—the bands of time
Not at once
It fought me, dug nests for its fellows in my body
I became a dwelling for wild birds
Amid a wasteland

Now the beautiful bird will live there
Curled in a tangle of breath
The rodent of the foundations

WHAT THE WORD SCRATCH CARVED IN MY LIPS

The birds were a net for souls, they were traps, they left no
   open sky.

OUR WAY

OF BEING IN DANGER

1966

Our way of being in danger is our way as poets

Inhabited which I am not a wasteland

At the crossroads of insects
And the birds that rise on feeding and those that turn-
ing swoop quickly to the ground
You listen. The invitations of earlier populations
Are the dark roads, the channels that must exist.
The overseeing of the works, to salvage the waters
Through underground openings, difficult passages hitting
the brambles
I retract. I force my wild body, plead with it
Pierced by the breeze from the passing birds, eaten away, my
body, full of channels
Where I communicate with the water

And my soul ascends upon the body's death
Which soon will be the beat of a wave in an awful sea
The ear may not hear it
But a whole terror of loss swells the rising of the soul

Then the sea came to my side
It faced me
A ready bed in my body a stillness now deep

The wind came in great gusts for many nights
Moving the dark. Madly it carried scents from all over
Opening gardens at my sides. Other times you saw seascapes
Cool on the shores lay those we remember
Unburned, unwithering
Springs gurgled then
From one fresh water eased into the sea tracing quiet paths
Where on fine days if you swim the water feels cooler
As stepping on a marble tile on a summer afternoon
You being hotter, the tile in shade, nestled in the grass
Some other breath seems to pass
And tugged by tranquility pushed by fear
Is how you feel when you encounter those currents

Obstructed water is better for the thirst of their sainted
   mouths

Transverse darkness slices a series of days
Not a star shines at night
The darkness of night is not
A bird of that sort. I have become
A sky crumbling from within, a glowing
Prey of foam. Before the deep waters
A lone diver studies before he dives
That sea of sky, and his one large eye is the source

The empty tree moved that way
The tree was unknown, descending stairs upon stairs
Twigs branches trunk, deep
And the good when they died a fresh line of verdant leaves

The surrounding land that drank no water was strewn with
mud calyces, tiny holes in the earth, soil finer around
the lips. So too do the ready dead of spring envelop
their tenderness

And while it may not have brought the weather, blowing
motionless, the tree was a raft. Amid gathering clouds
and clusters of bad weather I sailed around it, and as I
embarked its inky black birds

Flocked to me there. The newcomers' reign came quickly,
their shadows swiftly imposed as the others departed,
sundrenched in a landscape of flight though their bod-
ies were dark

In this tree where I sat for years as its sound rose I
listened, waited for it to be heard

Some became voices and others silence
Remember that, when the shadow
Passed over me

.

I myself never had many other voices

Because I dwell in the abyss as in my poem, always hidden,
dwells not a word but a sob

How many times hunched in his boat does the fisherman
list with it over the abyss

Fishing for the dark life of my soul

And when at last the fish rises seized on the bait it seems a
stream begins to run from the darkness to the waters

of the sea
                Where could you find for it seasons
In bloom, so many gardens brimming
With despair, with incredible eros
Now in spring as they spun slowly lifting the coolness
I sat at night and watched the gardens becoming
Deep in a way, reminding me of the listing embrace
Of all those who became lovers
Of a breathtaking fall that lasted
The whole of that deadly sky

And beneath the tree in its shadow many had gathered,
fleshless, heads dawning in the first depths of shade,
beloved faces fatigued by a vigil that likens a crew of
strangers to a vessel of heart

At that hour it seemed as if everything on land were a flower

The miraculous catch

These poor people ready whole days and nights, awaiting
with great patience whatever fish might drop to the
water's edge, having lost from their clothes the sign that
distinguished them and beneath

they were beardless, and seeing their craft a small cypress in
the sea entrusted themselves to it as if it were home and
they only passages in the currents of the sea

which though few in number seemed to hint of many more
to come, and they spread their arms as if flying, as if the
fish were birds beating their wings in a sea that dragged
currents

and their countenance looked evenly on such abundance,
as if in the mystery taking shape the shore stretched on
without end

The shore with the cypresses

Among sorrows they triumphed as in early spring new
    shoots sprout radiant among the other branches, the
    darker, the ones from before

It was a miracle how the branch quivered at its tip, bearing
    the slightest weight, you'd think it only light

And now half the treetops, as the light slices them, seem
    to you like a hovering flock of sheep that slowly and
    grazing proceed

This scene at a time of rest seemed also a gift to poets
With quiet desire their poems shine

In a deep dream that dreams another dream

Whatever happened was in the air
It touched me
Though for me perhaps an era had ended

The seasons' lamplighter guarding the graves ignites a line
      of trees
And I envision a return of the senses when the gift will be
      given
When love will be greater
As when you surpass desire and each sensation in eros
      becomes its own exquisite thing
And a share of the world goes
To the one that runs, the other that chirps
The world is full
As I would want and without
Taking fright that the mind sails

I believe whatever will no longer seem wondrous or strange
      may in that place come to pass

At the age of eros I faced the first mystery
If I can persevere
Celebrating the mystery of death
In a fragrant walk

The other remembers the body that offers such love

And the days are fine
In the cool low shade of the earth
Amidst which we walk
You see groups on outings
How modest nature is
I gather grasses and memory blooms
I speak of those I have known
I call them worries, I call them lambs
They were elsewhere and found us at evening
Did I write it: shepherd of waters?
And they find tasty food
For the meadows are salty

Lapped by the sea the countries migrated, and for them it
     became sky
And the grass wouldn't know their step
Nor walking could it be heard
Now I notice more, the ones that end fastest
Hold magic, brimming the soul
And how everything is offered them
And the poets see a sign in their
Way of being
Who are happy
They have no place to rest and must rise at dawn
Their vigil is god's great sleep at their side

Descending on my slow walk I felt verdant on this
spirited morning and the deep plashing of a swimmer
who comes early to a sea still waveless held my atten-
tion to the sound I heard within

I watched as one arm rising he turned, the next sliced the
water in rhythm, following, earning its length

And the world seemed to be learning midway through cre-
ation that one who is saved is a source, a sweet drop of
breath

The sea glistened like the spine of a fish, it felt like stroking a
sheep, your fingers sinking deep in its curly fleece, and
when it passed another would come following

As in a circle how low these shorelines greet the sky

They held the outline of a face, and it shone,
Whose sadness made it forever innocent

I first saw them bending to drink water

TRANSLATOR'S NOTE

"The Thing's Other is a Thing": Translating Eleni Vakalo

> *Now you'll see, I'll weave even more out of this, as*
> *listening to the foreign language I was deeply speaking*
> *our own, and came to understand how difficult it is for*
> *a person to name things truly*
>   *And it's another thing,*
> *as they said,*   *for you to come to my words*

—Eleni Vakalo

It is, in fact, another thing to *come to the words of*—or, to translate this idiom otherwise, *come to agree with*, or *come to understand*—one of modern Greece's most surprising, even confounding poets. It is quite another still to attempt to bring those words to readers reading in languages other than hers. Eleni Vakalo (1921-2001), born in Istanbul, raised in Athens, trained in art history at the Sorbonne, was not naive about the difficulty of navigating linguistic difference. The passage above is borrowed from her 1978 *Tou Kosmou*, whose title in Greek encapsulates both the insularity of its language and the global scope of its imagined reach: one might render its genitive as *of, about, for,* or *to*, while the scale of signification of *kosmos* stretches from the local to the universal, from *people* or *crowd* to *world* or *globe*. Translation is, of course, what allows Vakalo's work to be *of the world* in a broader sense, to reach audiences beyond her own linguistic community. And her poetry, informed by her deep reading of literary, philosophical, and art critical texts, implicitly participates in translingual, transnational conversations about what art and literature can be and do. Yet it is also intensely inward-looking in its disruption of conventional grammar and syntax, which render it resistant to familiar modes of translation. Greek flows from Vakalo's pen in fits and starts that seem to reflect a metaphysical worry about whether one can ever "name things truly" even within a single language.

Greek is an inflected language in which word endings indicate grammatical function. Writers can, if they choose, shuffle the constituent parts of a sentence, trusting these endings to clarify the relationships between words. Alternatively, writers can manipulate these elements in such a way as to push their texts to the limits of intelligibility—"breaking the rules," as Susan Howe wrote of Emily Dickinson, "just short of breaking off communication with the reader." In the six early poems presented in this volume, Vakalo does just that: she intensifies the particular forms of grammatical ambiguity available in Greek by recasting its syntax in unexpected ways. Her earliest poems eschew punctuation; later ones use it sparingly. In this absence of periods or question marks, sentences as such are few and far between. It is often difficult for a reader to know where a unit of meaning begins and ends. Enjambment runs rampant. Present active participles such as *following, watching, leaving, grasping, resembling*, normally rare in Greek precisely because of the ambiguity they invite, allow the poet systematically to obscure the subjects of her verbs: one might say that nearly *all* Vakalo's participles dangle. Her texts often exhibit mismatched numbers of subjects, objects, and verbs. "Digression about the spider" (which I might also have translated as "The spider's parenthesis") has no main verb, six present participles, three nouns in the nominative that could all be subjects, and several nouns that could operate as either subjects or objects—a cumulative uncertainty that, in my interpretation, reflects the very interpenetration of innocence and guilt the text describes. This is not an exceptional case, nor is it unrelated to the broader themes of Vakalo's poetry. Her work is full of blind eyes, failed attempts to understand, fragments of language dropped here and there that cannot be assembled into a logical whole. This poetry seeks out alternatives to conventional syntactical logic, narrative continuity, and even the building of comprehensible relationships between doer and deed. We might, then, see the eavesdropper in *The Forest*, who "never gathered from the debris" of others' whispered conversations "all he had imagined," as a figure for Vakalo's reader, who is invited to listen to a series of "voices / Foundered by decay" (*Diary of Age*) and make of them what she will.

The challenges posed by this sustained breach of linguistic conventions may explain why Vakalo—who received both the State Poetry Prize and the Academy of Athens Prize, and whose *Meaning of the Blind* was praised by critic Nora Anagnostaki as "one of the most important books of poetry ever to be written in modern Greek"—has yet to be widely translated. For my part, it has taken me over a decade to "complete" these translations, or rather, to finally let go of the exhilarating process of coming to Vakalo's words, coming to know her peculiar world, as "hugging the wall touching the objects one by one adjusting their positions I come to know them" (*Meaning of the Blind*), a phrase that is as apt a description of translation as any I know. Her work offers other such metaphors, too: a "new stalk / strong / and blooming / sprouts from the very root" of "Plant Upbringing," this time in a different language. The blind eyes of *Description of the Body* embed in the body of an English translation, "watching afterward from there." Yet this interlingual coming-to-her-words never culminates in an arrival. The translations I present here are less an end product than a resting point in a process that could easily have continued for another decade or more. Vakalo's work is a reminder that meaning is not found but made; translation, like any interpretive encounter, must always make that meaning anew, and could always make it otherwise. The oddness—but also, I hope, the peculiar beauty—of my English is necessarily other than the oddness and beauty of Vakalo's idiosyncratic Greek.

And of course "Vakalo's Greek" is not just one thing: the particular editions I chose to translate are, too, resting points in a history of production that both pre- and post-dates them. Vakalo published her first two collection of poetry in 1945 and 1948, in a Greece riven by the violence and fear of the Axis Occupation and the subsequent civil war. In the following decade, in the wake of this horror and after years spent in Paris, her work became more experimental, as she moved away from the idea of the "collection" toward book-length poems that utilized the space of the page and spread in visually innovative ways. When translator Kimon Friar wrote to Vakalo in 1960 to express his interest in including a few of her "most representative or best poems" in an anthology,

Vakalo drafted a response (in English) that stated the impossibility of extracting "poems" from her books: "The poems as you see are whole units in every of my books except in *Wall Painting* and that is the preferable way to present them." By this point, Vakalo had already decided to distance herself from her two early collections. Her own later accounts of her career treat *The Forest* (1954), with which I open this volume, as her first book; from *Wall Painting* (1956) she retained only "Plant Upbringing," also included here. Between 1959 and 1966, Vakalo composed four additional book-length poems that came to comprise an unfolding series to which she eventually gave the title *Before Lyricism*. The present volume adopts that name, and brings all six together under a single cover.

It is not, however, the first publication to do so: the poems were collected in Greek as *Before Lyricism* in 1981, and again as part of *The Thing's Other (Poetry 1954-1994)* in 1995. While *The Thing's Other* is the volume current-day readers would find in a bookstore, I chose to base my translations on the first editions, which were printed in tiny runs of 200 or 300 copies, and are now to be found only in libraries or private collections. This choice reflects an interpretive stance regarding the way these poems mean: the first editions, whose layout the poet herself designed, are not just linguistically but visually idiosyncratic, while the later collected editions intervene drastically in Vakalo's organization of her pages and spreads, condensing the text to fit on far fewer pages. The six book-poems I present here are what Andreas Karandonis described as "experiment-objects," which treat the book as a tactile object with features to be explored as elements of poetic composition. Her pages and spreads often display sprawling yet deliberate assortments of prose, free verse, and even rhymed and metered lines, a mixture of styles and registers that can be both heard and seen. Vakalo's interest in this aspect of poetry may not come as much of a surprise to those familiar with her work as one of the most important art critics and historians in twentieth-century Greece. She authored several books of art history and theory, as well as weekly columns of art criticism for a major Athenian newspaper for many decades (excluding the period of the dictatorship of 1967-74). In 1958 Vakalo and her husband—painter and stage designer Giorgos Vakalo, whose sketches and drawings feature in a few of her early books of poetry—founded Greece's first School of Arts and Design, where she taught for over thirty years. Vakalo was acutely aware of contemporary developments in the visual and plastic arts, and her ongoing commitment to art and design made her particularly attuned to the space of the page and the physical structure of the book as a whole.

I myself first encountered Vakalo's poetry almost purely *as* image or object, twenty years ago in the Rare Books and Manuscripts division of Princeton's Firestone Library. The library's holdings include drafts and first editions for all of Vakalo's books of poetry. At the time, my curiosity about Greek literature far outstripped my language skills, and I was unable to decipher much of the writing. From the start I thus encountered this body of work with a heightened awareness of the spatial deployment of text, the color of the ink, the shape, size, and heft of these handwritten books. To this day, the object I hold in my mind as an emblem of Vakalo's poetics is a 1971 date book of mahogany-colored leather containing an advanced draft of *Of the World*. The text is written in green ink, except for a few passages quoted from *The Forest* (1954), copied out in red. Vakalo treated each page as a visual field, placing bits of script at the top, toward the bottom, along the left-hand margin, or in the middle of the page; an occasional clump of text would be circled and moved via penned-in arrows. There was also a later typescript, and a copy of the first edition; even a purely visual comparison of the three made it clear how deeply involved the poet had been in the design of the eventual printed product. For Vakalo, composition was clearly not just about words. Some of the fair copies in the archive are even accompanied by instructions to the typesetters concerning the width of margins, the placement of page numbers, how prose and verse are to be kept typographically distinct, and which pages are to bear front and back matter. In one such note, Vakalo stresses the importance of adhering to the visual details of her fair copy: she has positioned the lines "at the height where they should be placed during printing," and asks "that these positions please be observed."

The present volume takes this request at its word: I make every effort to maintain the layout of pages and spreads within each work. This effort can, like so much about translation, be only a gesture, not a reproduction: after all, I am translating into another alphabet and a different typographic tradition, and bringing under a single cover six volumes whose first editions are a range of shapes and sizes. There are also other visual differences. For instance, the first edition of *The Forest* contains pen-and-ink drawings by Giorgos Vakalo that we were unable to include in this collected edition; the spreads have thus been redesigned to account for that absence. But the point of translation is not to reproduce, but to extend: this volume also continues the series of *Before Lyricism*, in some sense, by building on it in another language, building a *beyond* and an *after* for that *before*. "The thing's other is a thing," Vakalo wrote in her very last book of poetry, *Epilogue* (1999). Translation, too, is a kind of epilogue, an extension of a work in a new linguistic and poetic context, and in new and different experiment-objects. Translations always present others to the things they translate, and those others are themselves embodied things. To return to the passage I quoted in the epigraph above, I hope these translations do indeed "weave even more" out of Vakalo's poetic matter. I hope they allow us to move toward her words, while also inviting us to speak our own language more deeply, in part by listening to—and looking at—the foreign. I hope they help us, ultimately, to question the line between "our own" and "the foreign," by challenging the solidity of both.

A few deep thanks are in order, to individuals and institutions who supported this book. First of all, a National Endowment of the Arts grant in 2007 gave me necessary time off from teaching to begin my translations, which have been percolating ever since. Continued access to the Eleni Vakalo archive at Princeton was crucial to this project, and I am grateful to Firestone Library for allowing me to quote from unpublished material in this note. I am also grateful to Dimitri Gondicas of the Seeger Center for Hellenic Studies at Princeton for his steadfast support over these many years. The poems have had many readers, all of whom have given invaluable feedback: David, Helen, and Michael Emmerich; Peter Constantine, Emmanuela Kantzia, Sarah McCann, Nick Moschovakis, David Roessel, and Katerina

Stergiopoulou; Amanda Doxtater, Leah Middlebrook, Hilary Plum, and Casey Shoop; Ivi Kazantzi, Panayiotis Pantzarelas, and Theodora Valkanou. Andreas Galanos has been the most dedicated reader of all, sitting with me in a Brooklyn living room, a basement apartment in Washington, D.C., and cafés all over Greece, poring over each phrase in Greek and English both. Finally, Anna Moschovakis and Matvei Yankelevich have been the most patient of editors; I am grateful to their attention to each word and typographic detail.

Karen Emmerich
March 2017
Brooklyn, NY